HANDS ON

HOW TO USE BRAIN GYM® IN THE CLASSROOM

**Further books on Educational Kinesiology & Brain Gym®
available from:** Body Balance Books, 12 Golders Rise, London NW4 2HR
Tel: 020 8202 1732   Email: info@bbbooks.co.uk   Fax: 020 8202 3890
www.bbbooks.co.uk

Note from the Educational Kinesiology (UK) Foundation
Training in Brain Gym® is available throughout the British Isles and is recommended in
order to use the Brain Gym® activities with maximum effectiveness. For talks, seminars,
courses and details of your local Instructor, who can also offer individual sessions,
contact the EKF at the above address/fax or **Tel: 020-8202 3141 or email:
brain.gymgb@euphony.net or visit our website: www.braingym.org.uk**

Isabel Cohen and Marcelle Goldsmith
Based on the work of Paul E. Dennison, Ph.D., and Gail E. Dennison

Hands On: How to Use Brain Gym® in the Classroom

First edition published 2000 by "Hands On" Books, P. O. Box 1019, Sea Point 8060, South Africa. Copyright 2002, 2003 by Marcelle Goldsmith and Isabel Cohen.

This third edition printed in the United States of America. Brain Gym® is a registered trademark of the Educational Kinesiology Foundation, Ventura, CA, USA, edukfd@earthlink.net, www.braingym.org. The Brain Gym® and Vision Gym® movements, as well as many of the other processes described in this manual, were originated by Paul E. Dennison, Ph.D., and Gail E. Dennison, and are used by permission. Vision Gym® is a registered trademark of Paul and Gail Dennison. For information on the Dennisons' publications, go to www.braingym.com or email EduKBooks@aol.com. No part of this book may be used or reproduced in any manner whatsoever without written permission from the publisher, except in the case of a brief quotation embodied in a critical article or review. For information, please contact the publisher:

Edu-Kinesthetics, Inc.
P. O. Box 3395
Ventura, CA 93006-3395 USA
Email: EduKBooks@aol.com
www.braingym.com

To find a Brain Gym® Instructor in your area, contact:

Brain Gym International/Educational Kinesiology Foundation
(800) 356-2109 from the U.S. and Canada
and (805) 658-7942 from all other countries
edukfd@earthlink.net
www.braingym.org

This work retains the South African spellings and punctuation, with the exception of the names of the copyrighted Brain Gym and Vision Gym movements.

The procedures and techniques described in this book are solely for educational use. The authors do not intend to present any part of this work as a diagnosis or prescription for any ailment, nor do they take responsibility for anyone misrepresenting the program through such action.

Graphics, Typesetting, Layout and Design: Lizette Moskovitz
Cover design: Koleen Sargent-Murray and Lizette Moskovitz
Photos: Isabel Cohen and Marcelle Goldsmith
Drawings of eye and ear on page 77: Gail E. Dennison

ISBN 0-942143-12-4

A Message from Paul and Gail Dennison . . .

The teacher of today must be prepared to accept each child as a distinct individual with unique challenges and vast potential. When a teacher can meet a child where he is, honor that place, and guide the child to learn at his own pace for his own sense of intrinsic worth, true education happens. *Hands On: How to Use Brain Gym® in the Classroom* is a journey through the wonderful world of Brain Gym, a world where such true education is possible.

Hands On is intended as a companion work to our book *Brain Gym® Teacher's Edition*, which introduces this exploratory world of movement-based learning. Through their useful, photo-filled book, Isabel Cohen and Marcelle Goldsmith, teachers in the South African school system, have captured the joy of learning through movement for all of us to share.

The *Hands On* book gives informed teachers, parents, and occupational therapists practical, visual, step-by-step ideas on how to use the Brain Gym movements to support a child as she discovers reading, handwriting, spelling, or mathematical computation. If you've wondered how you might implement this work in your own life—or in your classroom to encourage your students' reawakening to the physical skills of learning—*Hands On* will get you started on an incredible adventure.

Parental involvement is essential to the success of the Brain Gym program, and teachers and parents have much to gain by experiencing this intrinsic learning for themselves before offering it to others. We hope that, after reading this book, you'll feel inspired to seek out a professional Brain Gym Instructor in order to deepen your understanding.

The value of movement is much greater than simply acquiring academic skills. Brain Gym is not a mechanized process or a therapy. It's a series of safe, natural movements that enhance learning by addressing the sensory elements involved in the integration of new ideas. Movement prepares us to teach ourselves. Starting with PACE, this book brings more play, movement, pleasure, and success into the learning process. The photos of children doing the Brain Gym activities are inviting, easy to follow, and inspirational. They help make *Hands On* an essential aid for every schoolteacher who uses Brain Gym.

Marcelle and Isabel are exemplary teachers: sincere, loving people who see only the best in others and know how to draw it out. We highly recommend them and their wonderful book, and are honored to introduce them to you.

Introducing

MARCELLE GOLDSMITH (BSc Occupational Therapy)

Marcelle qualified as an Occupational Therapist in 1989 at the University of Cape Town, South Africa, and has worked in the area of learning difficulties, among others, for more than ten years.

Her work in this area, and her keen interest in movement and dance, led her in 1995 to Educational Kinesiology, in which she qualified as a Brain Gym Instructor. She has since incorporated Brain Gym into all her work.

After having completed the Movement Dynamics course in Australia, Marcelle was inspired to create a course geared toward those with an interest in movement and dance.

Marcelle, together with Rita Edwards and the late Esta Steenekamp, developed the Brain Gym for Pre-Schoolers* course, following which she collaborated on the Brain Gym in the Classroom* course. (*courses taught in South Africa)

ISABEL COHEN (Diploma of Education TED, DSERE Unisa)

For more than 24 years Isabel has had a special interest in remedial teaching with learners of all ages having specific challenges such as dyslexia, mental and physical handicaps, and with adult learners recovering from head injuries.

The challenges involved in this type of work led her to Educational Kinesiology in 1993, and she has since qualified as a Brain Gym Instructor. She now uses Edu-K and Brain Gym integrally in all her teaching work.

Isabel's other passion is sport. After completing the Edu-K course Switched-on-Golf, she has introduced aspects of Brain Gym to professional cricketers and hockey players, and continues to develop this area of interest wherever possible.

HANDS ON represents the culmination of the authors' desire to share and network their knowledge and experience in the area of Brain Gym and Educational Kinesiology. Since its publication, Marcelle and Isabel have also been sharing a two-day, play-filled workshop for teachers, parents, and therapists, called "Hands On: How to Use Brain Gym® in the Classroom and Beyond," which uses this photo manual as its text. For more information about this workshop, visit www.braingym.org.

Acknowledgments

We wish to acknowledge the work of Paul E. Dennison, Ph.D., and Gail E. Dennison, the creators of Brain Gym and Educational Kinesiology, without which our work and manual would not have been possible. All the Brain Gym movements described in this book are based on *Brain Gym Teacher's Edition (Revised)* and *Vision Gym: Playful Movements for Natural Seeing*, and are reproduced here with permission.

We wish also to acknowledge Carla Hannaford, Ph.D., whose pioneering spirit brought her to Africa to teach us this work originally. Her book *Smart Moves: Why Learning Is Not All in Your Head* and her course Physiology of Brain Gym form the basis of our understanding of the neurophysiology of Brain Gym.

Further, we would like to acknowledge the teaching and guidance of the International and National Faculty Members of Southern Africa, notably Rita Edwards, the late Esta Steenekamp, and Melodie de Jager, who have greatly influenced the quality and direction of our work in this field.

We also acknowledge International Faculty members Pamela Curlee (USA), Gillian Johnson (Australia), and Gill Brooksmith (England) for their invaluable teaching; and Barbara Smith, Judy Grant, and the whole Foundation review team for their generous participation.

Our very special thanks go to our teacher and colleague Rita Edwards, International Faculty Member for Southern Africa, for her guidance, support, encouragement, and input during the past few years. She has taught us much, and in so doing has empowered us to embark on the **HANDS ON** project. We will always be grateful to Rita for starting us off on the exciting path of growth and learning with Brain Gym.

Our thanks go to the principal, Brian Bosworth, teachers, and pupils of Timour Hall Primary School in Plumstead, Cape Town, and to the principal, Cheryl Lazarus, and pupils of Vered Pre-Primary School, Camps Bay, Cape Town, for allowing us to share our ideas and capture classroom activities in photographs.

Thanks are due to Raymond Rudolph for his continual support and creative input. We also thank Gavin Goldsmith for his encouragement and help.

Our grateful thanks go to Lizette Moskovitz for her unending enthusiasm, tenacity, creativity, and belief in our project, and for her hours of work at the computer.

For her superb editing skills that have assisted Gail, Paul, and ourselves in producing a manual of quality, we thank Sonia Nordenson.

To all the children we have worked with and who have worked with us: We thank you deeply for teaching us.

This manual was born out of a desire:

To share our years of experience in, and our LOVE for, the work.

And so we dedicate this book to:

Scott Halliford, Donna Chait, Sián England, Russel Hall, Paul Rawraway, and Ahmed Wadee, who taught Isabel that "ceiling" is a word best left to the building trade!

Nichola Beyers and Quinton Maré, who showed Marcelle the meaning of "courage" and "joy."

Jodi Schaffer, who taught Rita and Isabel so much!

And the teachers and kids who use Brain Gym on a daily basis to make learning easy and fun.

Marcelle and Isabel

How to use this manual

Each of the Brain Gym® movements, though simple to do, provides entry to a rich world of learning support. To gain maximum benefits from the movements, seek the instruction and guidance of an Edu-K professional, who can help answer such commonly asked questions as: *What specific movements should be used for reading, writing, or spelling?*

HANDS ON: HOW TO USE BRAIN GYM® IN THE CLASSROOM has been designed to give the user practical, visual, step-by-step ideas on how to use the Brain Gym movements to develop skills of handwriting, reading, spelling, and math.

Chapter 1 - Readiness for Learning
This chapter introduces PACE and the various ways it can be done in the classroom (and elsewhere). Throughout *HANDS ON*, it is noted that PACE precedes all learning tasks.

Chapter 2 - Handwriting
Seven sub-skills for handwriting are identified and Brain Gym movements and their variations are suggested to develop these.

It is recommended that the users familiarise themselves with the individual movements as shown in the photographs. These can then be put together into workable (classroom) routines. We encourage creativity in the use of the movements - in other words, enjoy them!

Chapter 3 - Reading
This chapter offers activities and Brain Gym movements to help develop reading skills. Appropriate movements can be identified and used when needed.

Brain Gym movements to enhance the senses are highlighted on page 77. These are quick referrals for use when desired; for example: before a test, orals, or essay writing.

Chapter 4 - Spelling
In this chapter Brain Gym movements are combined with practical activities to enhance spelling skills. It is a very *HANDS ON* chapter for educators, parents, and learners to use at school and at home.

Chapter 5 - Math "teaser"
A few math skills are covered in combination with Brain Gym techniques, leaving the discussion open-ended for further suggestions from users.

Contents

Contents continued

The History of *HANDS ON*

About two years ago, we were both feeling a bit stuck as to how to share the wonderful work that Brain Gym is with our wider South African community.

There were several reasons for our frustration:

- We had noticed that people were doing Brain Gym courses yet were experiencing difficulties in applying this knowledge practically in the classroom, or in therapy sessions with learners.
- We wanted to expand the Brain Gym experiences for learners from our private practices into their school environments.
- We knew that Brain Gym is beneficial for all learners in all languages, whether socially advantaged or disadvantaged; having learning difficulties or not; younger or older; and in smaller or larger classes.

So we had the desire to get Brain Gym "out there" and into the classrooms of South Africa.

In thinking about how best to achieve this, the idea of a photo manual was born. We spent many months photographing learners in one-to-one sessions as well as visiting Timour Hall Primary and Vered Pre-Primary Schools. It has been a joyous journey, and it has only just begun. We have already forgotten the "labour pains"—hours of putting our ideas together in the manual format.

One of the roads has taken us to Khayelitsha, a bustling, disadvantaged South African community on the outskirts of Cape Town, where class sizes in some schools can reach as many as fifty pupils.

At the time of going to print, we have begun a *HANDS ON* Brain Gym outreach programme to introduce the teachers and learners of a Khayelitsha school to these playful movements that have had such a profound impact on our learners of the last eight years.

Both of us have been blessed to be able to share Brain Gym and Edu-K with our wonderful students. The shifts, improvements, and general development that has happened for our learners has been a source of constant joy.

We hope through this manual to share with as many people as possible the wondrous results that happen when Brain Gym is part of a learning process.

Marcelle and Isabel

The teachers at Ntwasahlobo Primary School in Khayelitsha, Cape Town . . .

. . . singing the PACE song in Xhosa—a world first!

Introduction

It's no secret that South Africa is facing enormous hurdles in its quest for peace, harmony, and prosperity. Perhaps the biggest hurdle of all lies in the educational arena. An effective educational system is certainly a key component of economic success. Our nation is in the process of revamping a system that was designed to undereducate the majority of our people. A key national challenge is to redress the vast inequalities that exist from one level of education to another, and to equip young South Africans with the skills to contribute to our economy and to provide for their families. If we do not work together as a nation and rise to these challenges, we will never take our place amongst the great nations of the world.

Knowing that education is the key to our future, and keenly aware of the vast disparities that exist, the Department of Education is continually searching for ways of enhancing our teaching system. A high priority in the classroom right now is to bridge the gap between the traditionally educationally advantaged groups and those previously disadvantaged. Curriculum 2005 and the move toward "outcome-based" education are some of the results of this quest. Another exciting discovery—and the subject of this manual—has been a learning enhancement technique called Educational Kinesiology (Edu-K), or Brain Gym, originally researched by Paul E. Dennison, Ph. D., and developed by Dr. Dennison and his wife, Gail E. Dennison. Brain Gym has proven to be successful around the world and has enabled children and adults of all backgrounds and abilities to learn more effectively.

More about Brain Gym®

Brain Gym is a series of simple body movements used to integrate all areas of the brain to enhance learning and to build self-esteem. The exercises can be done in just a few minutes and can be used by anyone. They are easy to do, and the benefits are immediate and obvious. For detailed descriptions of the movements used in this manual, see the books *Brain Gym*[6], *Brain Gym Teachers's Edition*[6], and *Vision Gym: Playful Movements for Natural Seeing*[2].

In the Edu-K philosophy, children are always invited—never forced—to move. For a number of reasons, children often unconsciously "switch off" the brain-integration mechanism necessary for efficient learning. For example, a child who experiences comprehension difficulties will tend to panic in the classroom. In this state the child will be unable to take in the lessons being taught. The movements of Brain Gym, used at the child's own natural pace, effectively help him or her learn to notice and "switch back on" into an optimal state for learning.

In technical terms, information is received by the brain stem as an "impress" but may be inaccessible to the front brain as an express. This inability to express what is learned locks the student into a failure syndrome. Whole-brain learning draws out the potential locked in the body and enables students to access those areas of the brain previously unavailable to them. Improvements in learning and behaviour are often immediate and profound as children discover how to receive information and express themselves simultaneously. The result is significantly improved education and performance.

Normal brain activity requires efficient communication among the functional centres located throughout the brain. When information cannot flow freely among these centres—usually because of stress—learning blockages occur. The Brain Gym movements facilitate the flow of information within the brain, restoring our innate ability to learn and function at top efficiency.

Brain Gym is used by teachers and therapists in intervention programmes for children with developmental and learning difficulties. The movements are so effective that they have been introduced in homes, businesses, and educational institutions in more than eighty countries on all seven continents. It's important for you to know that Brain Gym is only part of the vast Educational Kinesiology system, comprising hundreds of curriculum hours among its diverse course offerings on movement-based learning. The thousands of professional practitioners worldwide all began their studies with a basic Brain Gym course (if this interests you, see the copyright page for contact information).

The History of Brain Gym

The seminal research for Brain Gym was done by Paul E. Dennison, a pioneer in the field of applied neuroscience. Dr. Dennison based his discoveries on an understanding of the interdependence of physical development, language acquisition, and academic achievement. With a background in curriculum development and experiential psychology, he conducted research particularly into reading achievement and its relation to brain development.

Dr. Dennison spent nineteen years directing the Valley Remedial Center in California, and turning learning difficulties into successful growth. He and his wife, Gail Dennison, then developed a series of movements called Brain Gym that evolved into an effective learning tool for everybody—from athletes to schoolchildren to corporate executives.

The National Learning Foundation, which provides innovative solutions for American education, has selected Brain Gym as one of the top ten successful learning innovations in America. The Dennisons' work has also been honoured with the Reading Excellence through the Arts Award from RETA, a special interest group of the International Reading Association.

How does Brain Gym work?

The Dennisons describe brain functioning in terms of three dimensions of movement:
- Laterality
- Centering
- Focus

Laterality coordinates the left and right sides of the brain to communicate effectively, correlating to the Midline Movements; centering coordinates the top and bottom areas of the brain for organisation of thoughts and action, correlating to the Energy Exercises, and emotions correlating to Deepening Attitudes; focus coordinates the receptive brain stem with the expressive forebrain for comprehension and perspective, correlating to the Lengthening Activities. (See page 90 for the Brain Gym movement categories.) Brain Gym results in thorough integration of all these dimensions and leads to significantly improved performance.

Brain Gym contributes to the learning process by:

- Creating lifelong flexibility in learning.
- Enhancing perceptual motor skills to facilitate effective communication and academic abilities.
- Enhancing the ability to collect, analyse, organise, critically select, and evaluate information from a variety of sources.
- Promoting effective problem solving and responsible decision making through enhanced critical and creative thinking.
- Providing the skills to work independently and cooperatively as a member of a team/group/organization/community.
- Building confidence and self-esteem to enhance the ability to participate as responsible citizens in local, provincial, national, and global affairs.
- Developing effective decision making to enhance the ability to make wise and safe choices for healthy living.
- Developing empathy for others regardless of culture and race, thus enhancing the ability to demonstrate cultural and aesthetic sensitivity across a range of social contexts.
- Promoting self-empowerment and effective goal setting to enhance the ability to recognise the relationships among education, skills training, and career opportunities.
- Enhancing brain organisation, thus promoting appreciation of the link between mental concept and manual performance.

So...

Let's get ready to

(in the words of Paul Dennison)

"Learn to move

and

move to learn"

Chapter 1

Readiness for Learning

In Brain Gym, we call the first steps, "Get ready to learn", or simply **PACE**[4].

PACE stands for Positive, Active, Clear, and Energetic, which is how we need to be for whole-brain learning.

Carla Hannaford says in her book *Smart Moves: Why Learning Is Not All in Your Head:* "PACE stands for *Positive, Active, Clear* and *Energetic* learning. It is a learning readiness sequence that is usually done at the beginning of the school day, after recess and after lunch to effectively prepare the student for learning. I do it prior to any activity I want to be totally integrated for. It includes drinking water for energetic learning and then doing Brain Buttons, Cross Crawls, and Hook-ups."[9]

What are the PACE movements?

1. **E** = Energetic

Remember: sip small amounts of good-quality water throughout the day!

Water

Drink water—it is the most important inorganic substance in the body, and ideally the most abundant.

The brain is composed of almost 90 percent water, and needs to be kept hydrated.

2. **C** = Clear

Brain Buttons

In this movement we massage the Brain Buttons or K27s (the indentations between the 1st and 2nd ribs directly under the collar bone/clavicle to the right and left of sternum/breastbone) while holding the other hand over the navel.

This all helps to reestablish the organisation necessary for skills that involve crossing the visual midline (reading, writing, etc.).

3. **A** = Active

The Cross Crawl

There are many ways to do this movement. It always involves moving one arm and its opposite leg followed by the other arm and its opposite leg (the movement activates left/right, top/bottom, and back/front areas of the brain and body simultaneously).

4. **P** = Positive **Hook-ups**

Can be done sitting, standing, or lying down.

For Part One, cross left ankle over the right. Extend arms in front of you, left wrist over right and thumbs down, palms together. Interlace fingers and draw hands close to chest, elbows down. (Some prefer right ankle and right wrist on top.)

Now rest the tongue on the roof of the mouth behind the teeth and breathe in and out.

For Part Two, unhook feet and hands and place fingertips together and feet flat on the floor for a few seconds.

This has a calming and stress-relieving effect.

When and How We Do PACE in the Classroom

When?
- ✓ First thing in the morning
- ✓ After each break or recess
- ✓ Before sports activities
- ✓ Whenever we need to refocus—like before a test or exam

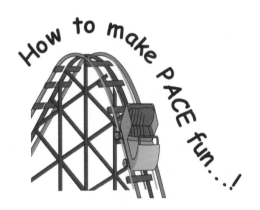

For Junior Primary Learners

PACE can be fun with these songs:
To the tune of "Frere Jacques":

1.

Let's drink water,
I love water.
It gives me
Energy.
Have some water too,
It is good for you.
Drink it up!
Drink it up!

2.

When I rub on
My Brain Buttons,
I see clear -
Far and near.
Do your buttons too,
It is good for you.
They clear you, and
Relax too.

3.

This is how I
Do the Cross Crawl:
Hand to knee,
Hand to knee.
You can Cross Crawl too,
It is good for you.
Activates and
Integrates.

4.

How I love to
Do my Hook-ups.
Calms me down,
Cheers me up.
Do your Hook-ups too,
It is good for you.
Helps us live more
Positive.

Are you in PACE yet?
Are you in PACE yet?
Let's go see.
Let's go see.
We'll do PACE together!
We'll do PACE together!
Come with me . . .
Come with me . . .

*(With thanks to Shirley Miekka,
Judy Metcalf, and
Bonnie Hershey for the words)*

Example of one verse to the tune of our South African "Shoshaloza":

Let's drink water,
I love water,
It gives me,
ENERGY
   ENERGY!
Have some water too,
It is good for you,
DRINK IT U-UP
   Drink it up
   Drink it up!

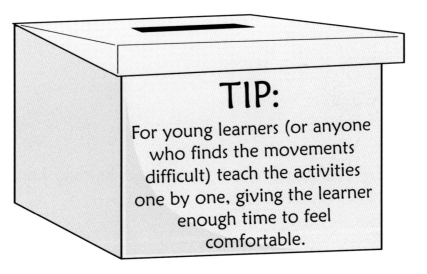

TIP:
For young learners (or anyone who finds the movements difficult) teach the activities one by one, giving the learner enough time to feel comfortable.

- Once learnt, the pictures of PACE can be placed in a bag, to be drawn out by a learner and practised until he or she is familiar with the PACE procedure.[10]

- At a later stage, when other Brain Gym movements are introduced, they may be added to the "Let's Get Moving" bag.

- Photographs can be taken of learners doing PACE and the Brain Gym movements and displayed in the classroom. (Other pictures and diagrams can also be used.)

Another song or rap

You make up the tune or just rap it!

1. Water:
H_2O is the thing to drink
H_2O is the drink to drink
H_2O is the one to drink
If you wanna
WORK and THINK!

2. Start by rubbing Brain Buttons and holding hand over navel:
Rub-a-dub-dub-dub-dubbidy dub
Rub-a-dub-dub-dub-dubbidy swap

(SWAP HANDS)

Rub-a-dub-dub-dub-dubbidy dub
Rub-a-dub-dub-dub (pause) dub dub!

3. The Cross Crawl:
Take your hand to the opposite knee
Take your elbow to the opposite knee
Take your shoulder to the opposite knee
That's the coolest Cross Crawl for you and me!

(Words by Marcelle Goldsmith and Isabel Cohen)

Try these to the tune of "Mambo No. 5," Lou Bega, by Prado P., Zippy, L. Bega,
©1999 Peer Music Publishers.

Young learners also enjoy doing PACE (and other Brain Gym movements too) in a story.

Some

to get you started:

Story One: The Spaceman

The Spaceman is getting ready for his journey into space. First he has a drink of water.

He puts on his helmet.

Then he fastens his helmet by rubbing his Brain Buttons. At the same time, he moves his eyes from side to side, while checking the panels.

Now he puts on his *heavy* space-suit like this: In a Cross Crawl movement he s-l-o-w-l-y puts his legs into the pants. Then he pulls the suit up, higher and higher each time, until he reaches his shoulders.

Then he climbs to the top of his spaceship (once again doing the Cross Crawl), reaching with one hand and the opposite knee.

He is ready for takeoff, but first he must check his computer.

Look at an **X**, displayed on a wall, or look at crossed fingers to "read computer screen."

He sits in his seat, calming himself and waiting for take-off (do Hook-ups).

Story Two: The Fairy Princess

The Fairy Princess wakes up, stretches, and drinks some dewdrops (water) from the nearest flower.

She still feels a little tired, so she rubs her Brain Buttons to clear her head. She blinks and looks all around while rubbing.

Standing up, she shakes the leaves from her beautiful skirt while swinging her arms from side to side across her body.

Then she puts on her Bracelets and Rings, gently rotating each arm, then the fingers, with the other hand.[2]

She now gets ready to float away by standing in Hook-ups (crossing her wrists and ankles). Then, opening her wings, she flutters off into the mist. As she lands at her destination, she places her fingertips together to rest.

TIP:

Create a "Getting Ready" or PACE story using the theme of the week, e.g., climbing trees to pick fruit or being a butterfly.
Also have mugs and water available in the classroom.
Water bottles are useful, too!

For Older Learners

When?
- ✓ First thing in the morning
- ✓ After breaks
- ✓ Whenever we need to refocus

To make PACE more fun for older learners, offer water and do Brain Buttons and the Cross Crawl to "The Brain Gym Rap" or to music. Lastly, do Hook-ups.

The Brain Gym Rap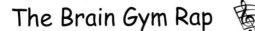

Rap, zap, don't take a nap!
Fun, free, see what you can be.
Move, groove, whatcha got to lose?
Spin, grin, everybody wins.

Set yourself a goal.
Break out of your role.

PACE, PACE, PACE the human race!
See for yourself
With a Happy Face.

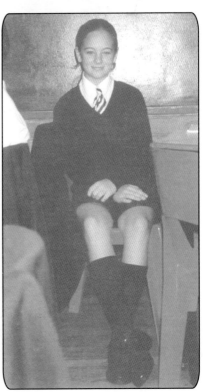

(With thanks to Rhonda Robles, Valerie Thomas, Catherine Warrick, and Donna Sewell for the words)

Use *music* (age-appropriate and **their** choice!)—this will make it much more fun!

As the children get used to the process, let them make up different moves for the Cross Crawl, as long as the opposite arm and leg are used in the movement. Marching, even though it doesn't cross the midline of the body, is a Cross Crawl variation.

Variations of the Cross Crawl[3] for All Learners

The Baboon

The Ankle Touch

The Hopscotch

The Cross Country Crawl

PACE can even be done sitting at a desk. It doesn't always have to be done together with the whole group. Sometimes a learner may feel the need to refocus, and can do these PACE movements solo; for example, before a test.

The March

An assisted **Cross Crawl**

On the Subject of Hook-ups

Part One of Hook-ups may be done in many ways; choose one that is comfortable for the learner.

The Dennison Hook-ups

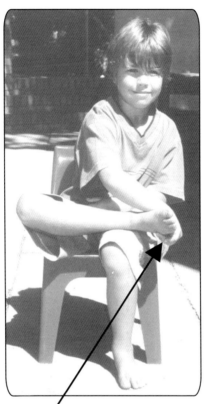

Cook's Hook-ups*: One hand over sole of the foot, then . . .

. . . one hand over top of the foot to join fingers of the other hand.

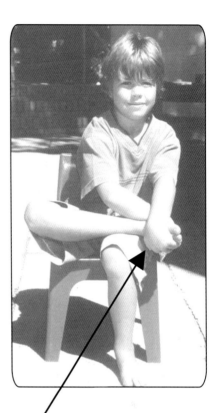

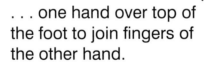

Above and right: Variations on the **Dennison Hook-ups**

* Developed by Wayne Cook

Chapter 2

Handwriting

Readiness for writing requires the development and practice of a number of different skills.

These are:
- ✓ Postural control
- ✓ Shoulder girdle stability and neck relaxation
- ✓ Finger strength and dexterity
- ✓ Visual skills
- ✓ Spatial orientation, including sizing and formation of letters
- ✓ Crossing the midline for writing
- ✓ Eye-hand coordination

**The PACE procedure can precede any learning activity.
So start with PACE!**

We need to sit correctly for a writing activity, so we must develop:

Postural Control

If some of these exercises need more space than is available in the classroom, include them in other lessons (for example, physical education).

Cross Crawl Sit-ups
(on a padded surface)

Opposite elbow to knee.

Shoulders can be lifted.

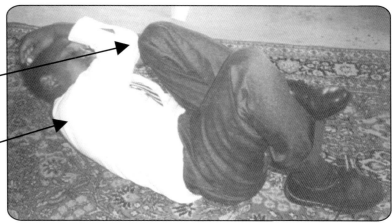

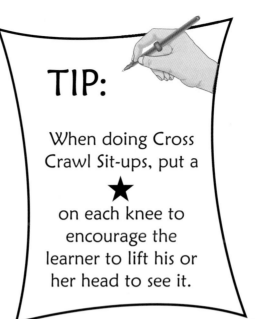

TIP:

When doing Cross Crawl Sit-ups, put a

★

on each knee to encourage the learner to lift his or her head to see it.

The Rocker

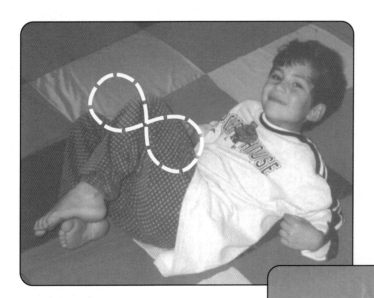

On a padded surface to protect the tailbone: Resting on elbows, trace a Lazy 8 with knees or rock from side to side.

The Caterpillar[2]
(Head slightly lifted)

Bend knees. Slide
backwards, with
opposite shoulder/hip
movements, until knees
are straight. Repeat.

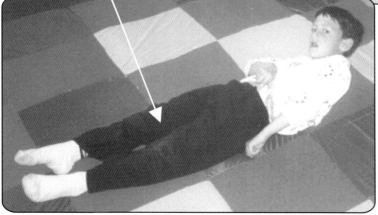

TIP:

Can be done as
a "caterpillar
race."

We also aim for:

Shoulder Girdle Stability and Neck Relaxation

Choose from these Brain Gym^6 and Vision Gym^2 exercises.

Neck Rolls

Lift shoulders. Place ear on shoulder.

Slowly roll head forwards and then to other side, where ear touches other shoulder.

Protect the neck by not letting the chin pass either end of the clavicle.

Repeat these movements with the shoulders dropped.

The Owl

Squeeze the shoulder muscle with the opposite hand.

Move head slowly to one side as you breathe in. Make a sound like the "whoo" of an owl, as you exhale looking over the shoulder. Repeat to the other side.

Lazy 8s

Trace a Lazy 8 with your hands: up the middle and round to the left, up the middle and round to the right. Move this way repeatedly, using right hand, then left, and then both hands together. Or trace a Lazy 8 with your nose. Lazy 8s can also be done while blinking, on a vertical surface (blackboard), or, using sticks and ribbons, to make large movements.

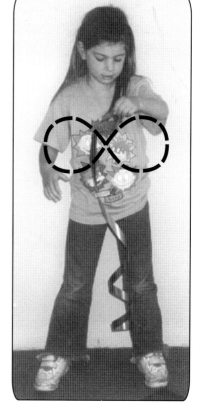

 See Appendix 4 and 5, pages 99 and 101, for Lazy 8 templates.

Elbow 8s[2]

Draw Lazy 8s or vertical 8s with each elbow in turn. Focus gaze on the elbow as you turn your upper body to the rear, finally centering the Lazy 8 over the middle of your tailbone.

The Elephant

"Glue" ear to shoulder and raise the arm on the same side.

Stand with feet hip-width apart, knees slightly bent.

First use one hand, then the other, to trace a big ∞.

It's natural to see a double image of your hand as you look past it.

Shoulder 8s

 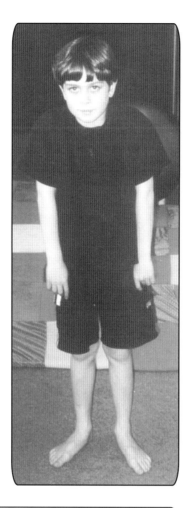 

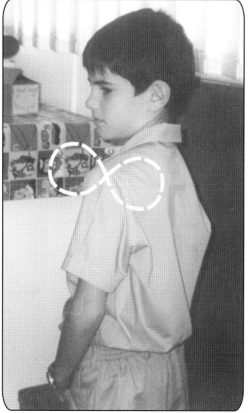

Trace the ∞ movement with one shoulder (left) or both together (above).

Wings[2]

Both elbows simultaneously trace the ∞ movement, hands meeting in the forward position and arms opening, winglike, as the back half of the 8 is traced.

Lazy 8 variation

Kneeling on all fours, use one hand to trace a ∞ on the floor while leaning on the other arm. Swap over and do the same with the other hand.

The Rainbow[2]

1. Arms out to the sides. Breathe in and look past your hand for a pot of gold.

2. Breathe out as you drop your head forward.

3. Repeat Step 1 to the other side.

The Calf Pump
Push against a wall or a partner.

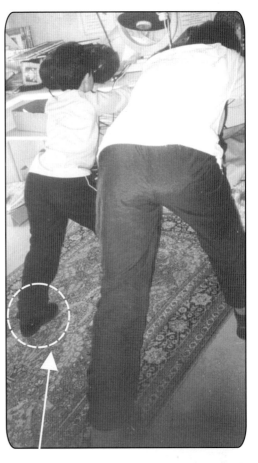

Lean on bent front leg.
Lift back heel, breathe in.

Gently lower your heel and
breathe out, then reverse.

The Calf Pump can also be done in pairs.

Arm Activation

Can be done with a partner.

Arms extended.

One partner gently pushes, the other resists*. Push partner's forearms downwards, upwards, inwards, and outwards.

Arms can be raised above the head.

Or do Arm Activation individually.

REMEMBER:

Use only a few of the exercises each time . . . Choose different ones and have fun!

Push against: back of arm

outside of arm

front of arm

inside of arm

*Avoid pushing on wrists.

Essential for writing is:

Finger Strength and Dexterity

Choose from these exercises.

Rings and Bracelets[2]

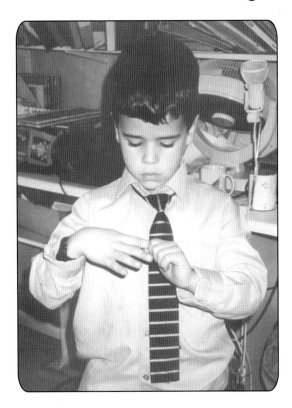 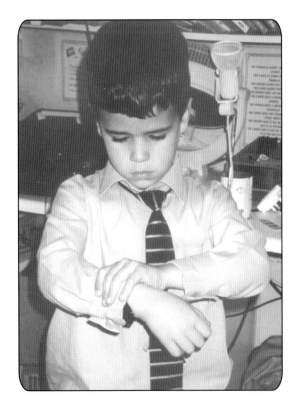

Twist around each finger . . . and arm.

Flicking and Clicking Fingers

Do the exercise in the shape of a Lazy 8.

Triangle 8s

While pressing fingertips together, trace the ∞ in the air.

Chain 8s

Grasp fingers of one hand with the fingers of the other hand.

Pulling them apart, trace the ∞ in the air.

TIP:

In all the Lazy 8 exercises described previously, the eyes can follow the ∞ movement.

We also need a relaxed yet focused visual system for writing. The following movements will help to develop:

Visual Skills

The "Buttons" movements

Brain Buttons

Fingers below collarbone (see page 6).

Eyes move from side to side.

Hand on navel.

Earth Buttons

Breathe in;
look up.
Breathe out;
drop eyes
downwards.

Fingers touch the chin.

Other hand faces down,
palm over the navel.

Space Buttons

The other hand rests in the lower back area.

Breathe in; look far.

Breathe out; look at
something close.

Fingers of one hand
rest or touch just
above the upper lip.

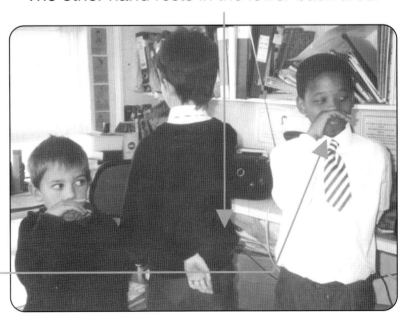

Balance Buttons

Three fingers press lightly on the back of the curved bone behind the ear.

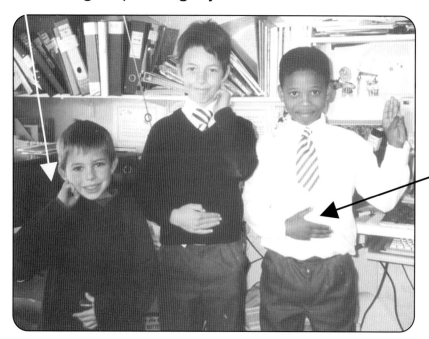

One hand over the navel.

Eyes look up to the right, down to the left; then up to the left and down to the right.

Breathe normally and then swap hands.

TIP:

For the BUTTONS exercises, do at least three eye movement sequences before changing to the other hand.

Lazy 8s for Eyes

Thumbs

Infinity 8s[2]

Triangles (p. 33)

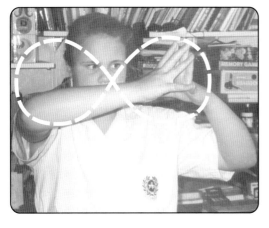

With all these exercises, the eyes follow the hand movements.

Triangles

Ribbons (p. 25)

Finger Puppets

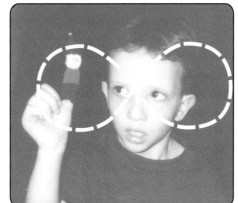

Ribbons

The Elephant (p. 26)

Look past your hand into the distance.

More Lazy 8s for the Eyes

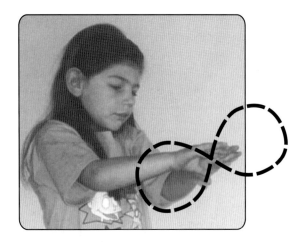

Making ∞s with bubbles

Dip bubble wand into liquid and trace ∞.

Chain 8s

Grasp fingers of one hand with the fingers of the other hand.

Pulling them apart, trace Lazy 8s in the air.

Tracing ∞s on a desk

Other Excellent and Useful Eye Tune-ups

Wake-up Points[2]

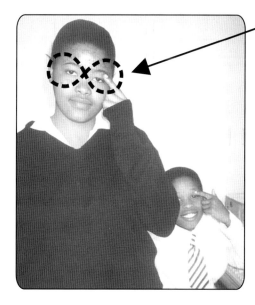

Press points around eyes, using fingertip.

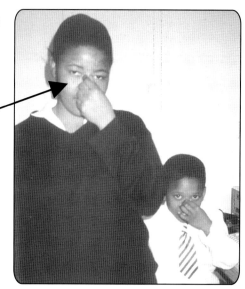

Lastly, pinch the bridge of the nose.

Heliotropic Breathing[2]

Breathe in, closing your eyes.
Breathe out, opening your eyes, and blink.

Butterfly Blinks[2]

Blink eyes while watching your hands do Double Doodles in the air.

As you blink, touch thumb to each fingertip to release tension from pencil holding.

Double Doodles

Draw the same pattern with both hands at the same time, in mirror image.

Soft Edges[2]

Hold moving fingers in front of eyes.

Focus on fingers, then look between them into the distance.

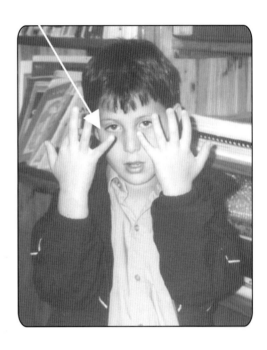

The Energy Yawn

Gently massage the points close to the ears where the jawbone moves.

At the same time, open the mouth in a big yawn.

Windows[2]

See what you discover!

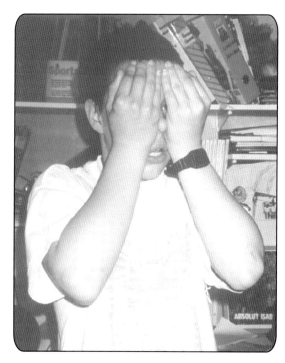

Cup hands and place them over eyes. (Fingers on forehead, hands resting on cheekbones.)

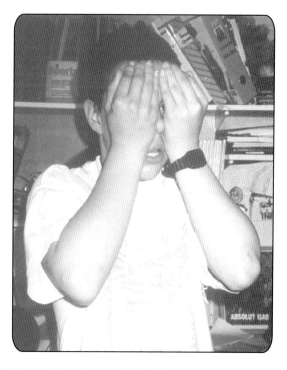

Breathe in and look up; breathe out and look down. Wink alternate eyes, then look at the darkness of the palms.

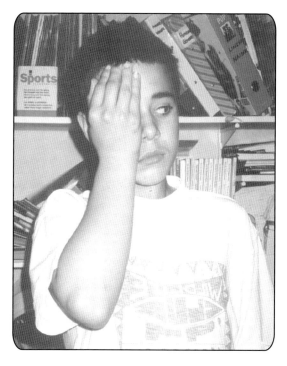

Remove one hand.
Both eyes explore what they can see out of the "window."

Repeat with the other hand.

The formation, sizing, and spacing of letters is also dependent on adequate:

Spatial Orientation

Using the following three Brain Gym movements can help to develop writing skills.

The Double Doodle

Can show learners how to use the width of the whole page, from margin to margin.

Draw Double Doodles on a magnetic board.

Draw the same pattern with both hands at the same time in mirror image.

Draw Double Doodles with crayon on paper.

Writing 8s

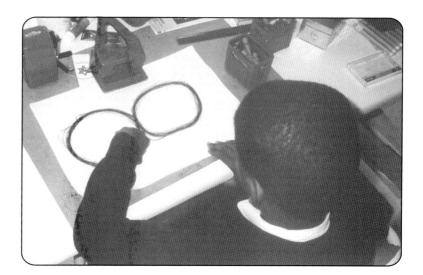

Start at 2 o'clock,
first with one hand . . .

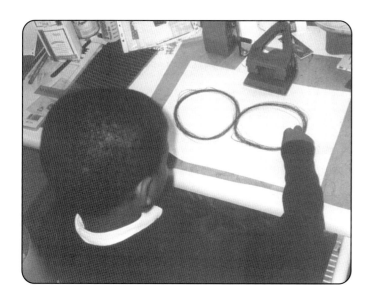

. . . then with the other hand.

Now use both hands.

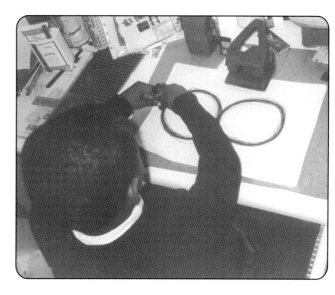

IMPORTANT NOTICE

Note the shape of the **Writing 8s,** which differ from the
Lazy 8s.

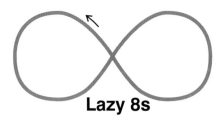

Writing 8s

SAY: Start at 2 o'clock on the left
side. Bounce round, up the
middle, and round again.

Lazy 8s

These exercises can be done large-scale on blank pieces of paper, on a
blackboard with chalk, or simply by tracing your fingers over the surface
of a desk!

For proper spacing between the lines, draw the writing s so that
they touch the lines at both top and bottom.

For example:

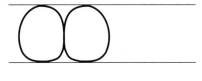

or

To show learners how to use the width of the whole page, from margin to
margin, use Lazy 8s in the following exercise.

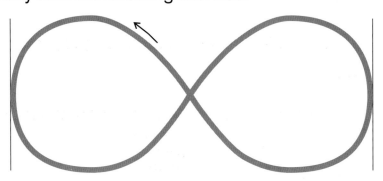

Alphabet 8s

The Writing 8s on the last two pages provide the basic shape used to form the Alphabet 8s. This next movement is fundamental to include in routines that practise the formation of letters.

Each letter of the printed, lowercase alphabet fits into the Writing 8s and can be practised as a single unit, in a group, or in an alphabetical sequence[5].

The letters can be drawn on blank or lined paper, on a blackboard, mat, or desk, or just in the air. See page 46 for a chart of the Alphabet 8s, and examples of how to fit the letters into the Writing 8s.

Here are some suggested cues to use with learners as they practise the formation of lowercase printing:

Start with the "2 o'clock" letters on the left-hand side of the Writing 8s, c o a d g q s e, and use the following verbal reinforcements.

c - Start at 2 o'clock, bounce round, but don't close the door.

o - Start at 2 o'clock, bounce round, and close the door.

a - Repeat sequence for o, and up stop, down stop.

d - Repeat sequence for o, and up up stop, down down stop.

g - Repeat sequence for o, and up stop, down down, and bounce round.

q - Repeat sequence for o, and up stop, down down stop, and flick.

s - Start at 2 o'clock, bounce round, slide, and bounce round again.

e - Straight across stop, bounce round and round (but don't close the door).

How to Use the Alphabet 8s

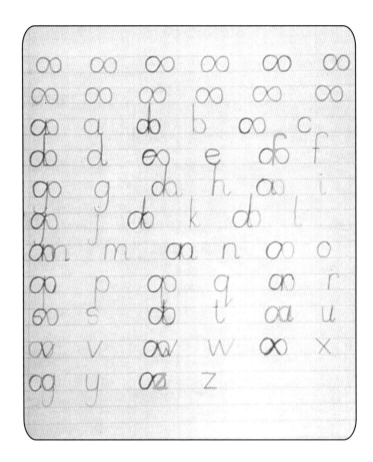

Start by doing the Writing 8s a few times. As the verbal directions on pages 45-47 show, the letters can now be incorporated into the shape of the Alphabet 8s.

So . . . then then two Writing 8s and then another letter

The photograph on page 47 shows Alphabet 8s being formed.

Every letter in this group begins with a curve and is formed on the left-hand side of the Alphabet 8s: c, o, a, d, g, q, s, e.

Now use these verbal directions with this group of letters that start on or near the midline and, in some cases, curve up and around to the right:

i r n m l h b p f

i - Straight down stop and add a dot.

r - Straight down stop, climb up, and bounce.

n - As for r and all the way down.

m - As for n and climb up, bounce, and down again.

l - Straight down stop.

h - Straight down stop, climb up, bounce, and down.

b - Straight down stop, climb up, bounce round, and close the door.

p - Straight down down stop, climb up, bounce round, and close the door.

f - Start to the right of the midline, bounce round, down down stop. Give him a bow tie.

Now comes **k**, **t**, and **j**

    k - straight down stop, (climb up), slide out-in, out-in.

    t - straight down down and bounce round to the right.

    j - straight down down and bounce round.

REMEMBER

Do some Writing ∞s in between each letter.

Now form **u** and **y**

    u - bounce down and up, straight down stop.

    y - as for **u** and, straight down and bounce round.

We find that these fit best into the right side of the Alphabet 8s.

Lastly, form these more angular letters on the right-hand side of the Alphabet 8s:

    v   w   x   z

To Improve Spacing, Use ∞s Between Written Words

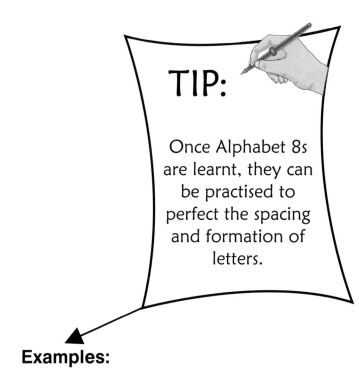

TIP:

Once Alphabet 8s are learnt, they can be practised to perfect the spacing and formation of letters.

Examples:

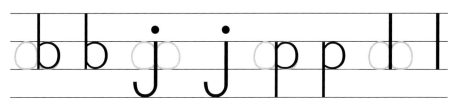

Crossing the midline is as essential for effective handwriting as it is for all other visual motor skills.

Crossing the Midline

All Lazy 8 movements and variations assist the learner to work across the midline. Here are a few reminders and additional suggestions:

- Lazy 8s with thumbs in the air
- Lazy 8s or Writing 8s on paper, board, in the air, on a mat, with crayons, shaving foam, sand, finger paints, etc.
- Alphabet 8s
- The Elephant
- Elbow 8s done in front of the body
- ∞s with streamers or ribbons on sticks

Lazy 8s and ∞ Exercises

With Ribbons

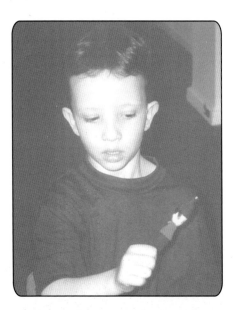

With Finger Puppets

More Exercises

Elbow 8s in Front

With Shaving Foam

On Chalkboard

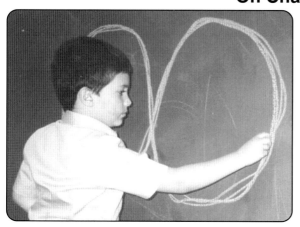
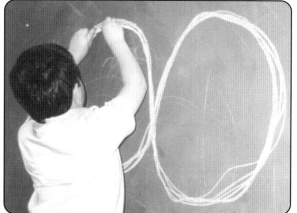

With Crayons

With Pavement Chalk

The Double Doodle is another Brain Gym movement that helps to establish the crossing of the midline. Simply put, a Double Doodle is a drawing. It uses *both* hands, drawing the same thing at the same time on opposite sides of the page, in a mirror image.

The Double Doodle can be done in many fun ways. Here are some examples, but do explore some of your own: with chalk on a blackboard or on the pavement; use your fingers in the air, on the desk, or on the floor; do them in the sand.

Use shaving foam on tiles

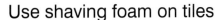

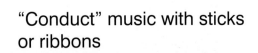

"Conduct" music with sticks or ribbons

Double Doodle on paper using crayons, pencils, finger paint, or pastels

All forms and variations of **The Cross Crawl**[3] help the learner to cross the midline.

The Cross Country Crawl

Marching

Elbow to Knee

Cross Crawl Sit-ups

Karate Kick Cross Crawl

Swing-Along Cross Crawl

It goes without saying that every learner, in order to develop good writing, should have well-established:

Eye-Hand Coordination

All the Lazy 8 movements and Double Doodles will help, as will the visual, finger dexterity, and shoulder girdle exercises previously described.

We know that there's a lot of information in this chapter. Just relax and breathe.

TIP:

Get used to the exercises one by one!

When you feel comfortable with these, start putting them together in useful routines (Tune-ups), depending on the time, space, and materials available.

REMEMBER

Brain Gym can be used anywhere, with no special equipment or space needed—just a few minutes of your time.

Tune-up Routines

We have devised a few Tune-up routines for you to experience, once you're more familiar with the basic movements.

PACE +

THE ROCKER - p. 22

NECK ROLLS - p. 24

RINGS AND BRACELETS - p. 32

EARTH BUTTONS - p. 35

WRITING 8s - p. 44

PACE +

CROSS CRAWL SIT-UPS - p. 21

THE OWL - p. 25

FLICKING AND CLICKING 8s - p. 32

THE ELEPHANT - p. 26

WRITING 8s BETWEEN LINES - p. 44

PACE +

THE CATERPILLAR - p. 23

ARM ACTIVATION - p. 31

CHAIN 8s - p. 33

LAZY 8s WITH EYES - p. 37

ALPHABET 8s - p. 45

Now create some of your own Tune-ups or pick out movements from the "Let's get Moving" bag (refer to page 9) and notice the changes!

The Bridge into Cursive Writing[5]

The slanted Lazy 8 can be used in the learning of cursive handwriting skills, as it helps the learner to integrate the direction, shape, formation, flow, and linking of the letters, thus serving as a bridge into cursive writing.

Slanting the Lazy 8

"The Lazy 8 becomes a preparation for cursive writing as the student learns to slant the midline to the right, creating a "cursive 8." Ideally, this Lazy 8 becomes automatic, fluid, and connected before the separate distinctions of the alphabet are taught."[3]

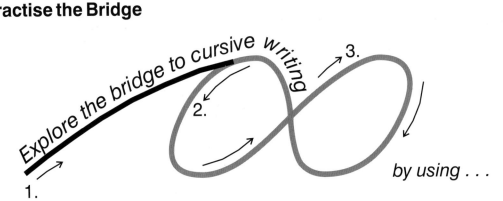

To Practise the Bridge

Explore the bridge to cursive writing
1.
2.
3.
by using . . .

. . . the "travelling" version of the Lazy 8 as follows:

Start with the bridge and a cursive C . . .

. . . continue and complete a slanted Lazy 8 . . .

. . . trace around the left side of the Lazy 8, leading into a second bridge and cursive C; then complete another slanted Lazy 8 and continue "travelling" the slanted Lazy 8 pattern.

The Cloverleaf

The Cloverleaf helps in the practice of continuous flow for cursive writing.

As with the Writing 8 on page 44, start at 2 o'clock, and bounce round to the left.

Now climb up to make a vertical 8 (remember, it is written in the same way as an 8, but is not as wide and is slightly slanted).

Then complete the right side of the Lazy 8.

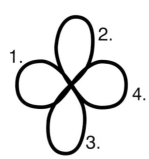

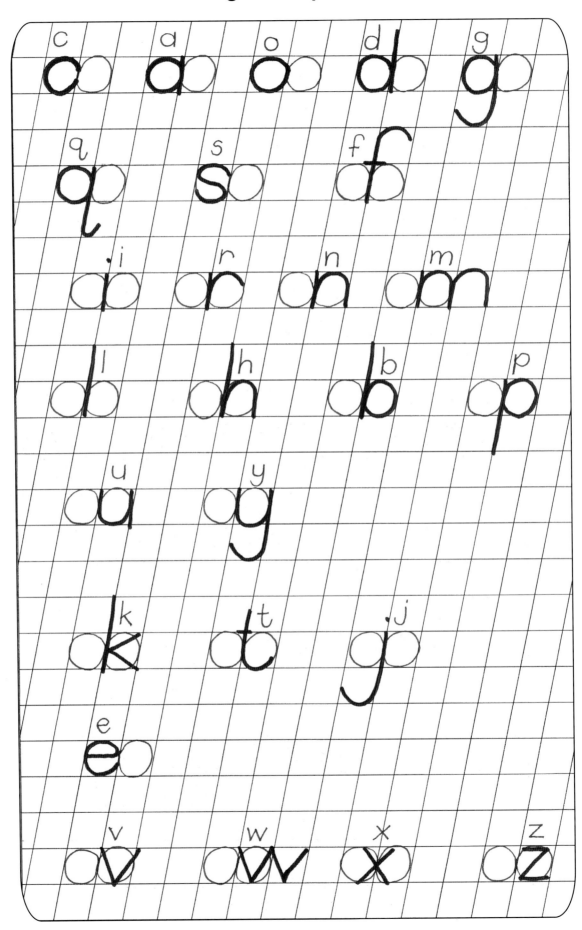

Cursive Writing with the Cloverleaf*[5]

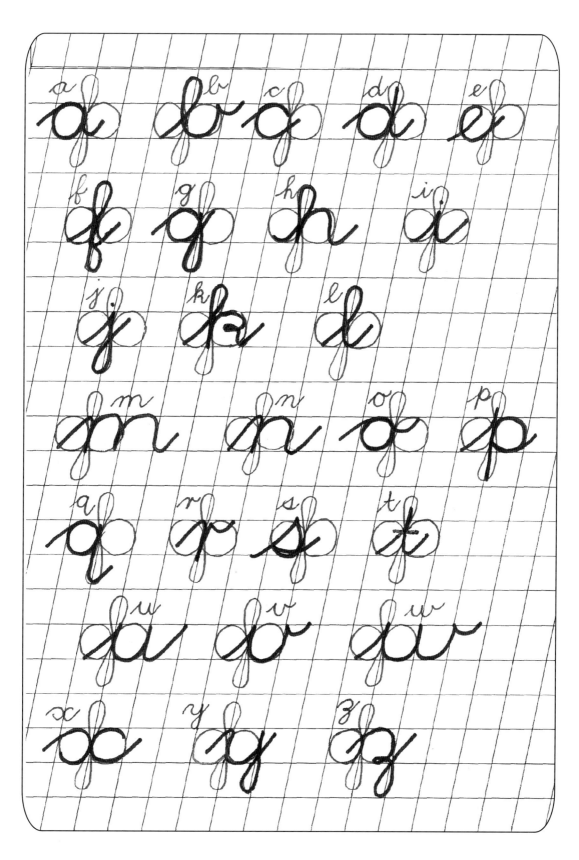

*From *The Dennison Approach to Whole-Brain Learning*
Note: First do a Cloverleaf, then complete a letter.

Cursive Writing in Alphabet 8s*

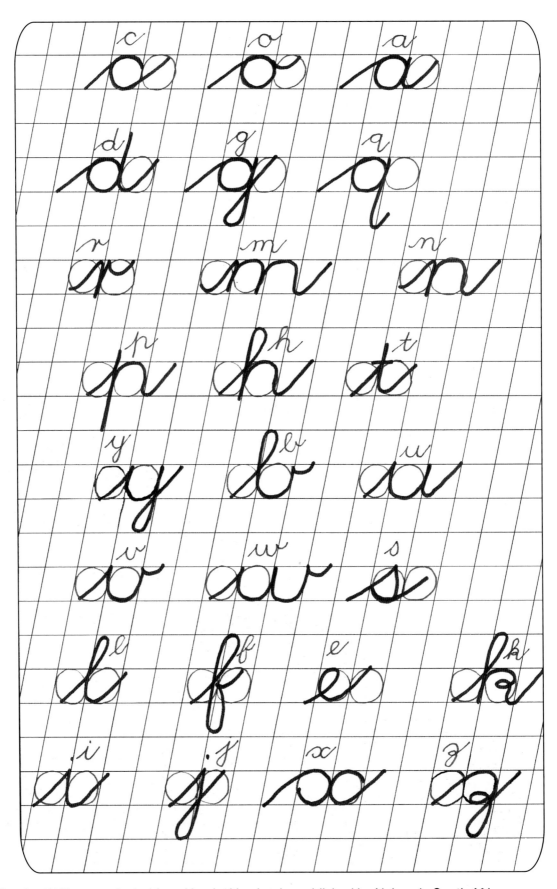

*Cursive Writing as adapted from Handwriting books published by Nelson in South Africa

Chapter 3

Reading

"Reading is to the mind what exercise is to the body."
—Sir Richard Steele

Reading is **decoding** the writer's message. We help learners to do this actively by building a number of vital skills.

Now, let's explore how we use the Brain Gym movements "hands on" in the classroom to do this.

Begin with PACE . . .
make it a *HANDS ON* habit!

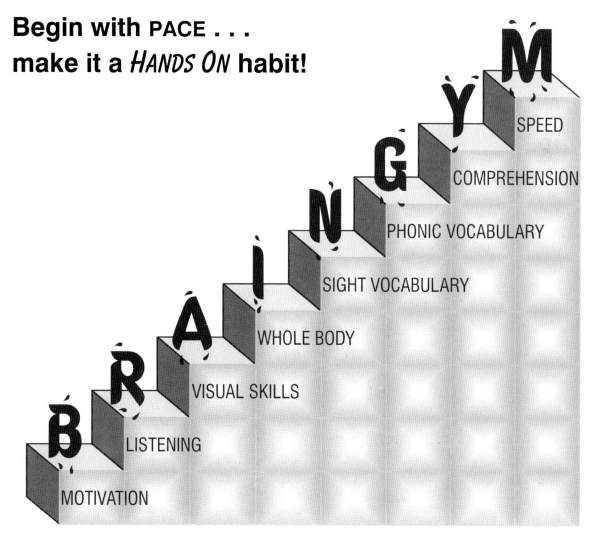

Skills for Reading

Motivation

Stimulate the desire to read by surrounding learners with fun, interesting, and age-related reading material and creating safe spaces in which to read:

- ▢ reading corners
- ▢ bookshelves
- ▢ flash cards
- ▢ magazines
- ▢ newspapers and clippings
- ▢ sports magazines
- ▢ their own books
- ▢ library books
- ▢ books with companion tapes
- ▢ label objects around the classroom

TIP:

Use the Positive Points with Hook-ups in PACE to increase motivation.

Hook-ups with Positive Points

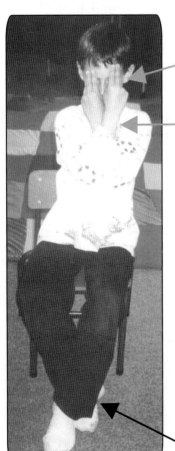

Lightly hold points.

Cross wrists.

Be excited about reading. Share this with the learners. Read to and with them. Enjoy it, and they will too!

Cross ankles.

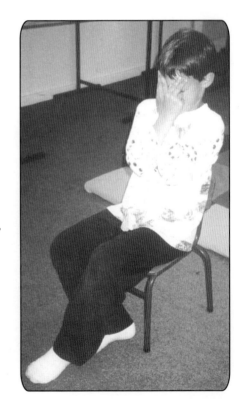

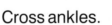

Some Brain Gym movements that improve listening skills are:

The Thinking Cap

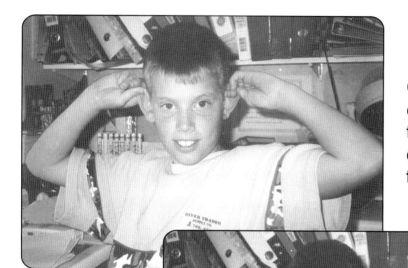

Gently unroll the outer edges of the ears from the top down to the earlobes. Repeat two or three times.

said

Put on your Thinking Cap while practising sight words.

The Elephant

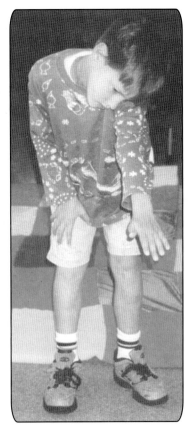 

"Glue" ear to shoulder.

Stand with legs apart.

Trace a BIG ∞ in front of the body.

Neck Rolls

Shoulders up, ear on shoulder, roll head from side to side: forwards and then to other side.
Shoulders down, repeat movement a few times.

The Energy Yawn

Rub points at jawbone and open mouth in a big yawn.

The Calf Pump

1. Lift back heel.

2. Bend front leg and gently lower back heel. Breathe out.

The Calf Pump with a partner

The Footflex

Hold at Achilles tendon; below the knee and . . .

point

and

flex the foot.

The Gravity Glider

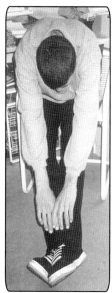

Sitting, cross one ankle over the other and reach down.

Swap ankles.

The Owl

Squeeze opposite shoulder muscle while slowly turning head three times to either side and making a sound like the "whoo" of an owl. Repeat with other shoulder.

To cross the visual midline for reading . . .

Lazy 8s with Thumbs

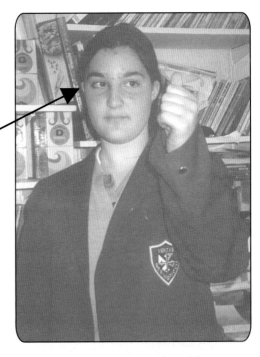

Eyes follow thumb.

Trace a with one hand. Then use the other hand.

Lastly, cross thumbs and trace with both hands together.

Do **The Infinity 8s** with closed eyes

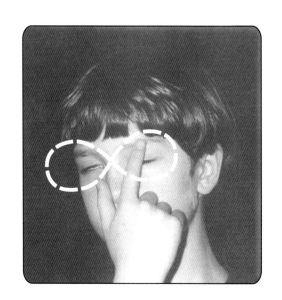

Trace ∞ around eyes with fingers.

Eyes follow under lids.

The Cloverleaf[2]

Draw a cloverleaf.

Eyes focus on centre point.

Nose traces the ∞ . . . then an 8 pattern:

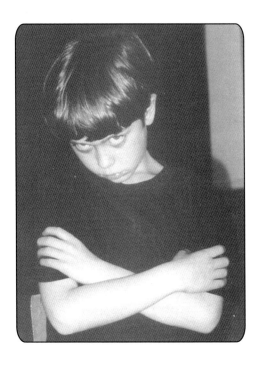

With folded arms, repeat the Cloverleaf

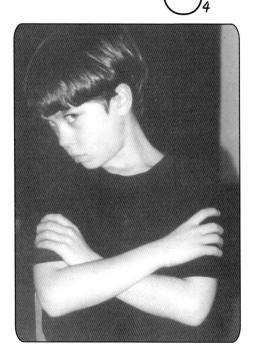

All the Buttons (Energy Exercises)

Brain Buttons: Move eyes from side to side (see p. 6).

Earth Buttons:
Breathe in, eyes up.
Breathe out, eyes down.

Space Buttons: Look far . . . look near.

Balance Buttons: Look up to the right, down to the left . . . then up left and down right.

The Energy Yawn

Look at an X:

Each learner can put an **X** on his or her desk. Also have a big **X** on the classroom wall.

The **X** helps to integrate eyes and brain.

Bubble Fun for the Little Ones[8]

In a group, one person blows bubbles. The others trace circles or Lazy 8s around the bubbles.

Pretend that your nose has a sharp point and point it at the bubbles till they pop. Or be an elf chasing the bubbles with your nose, elbows, or fingers by tracing an X or ∞ over them.

To develop good eye movement skills for reading, do these activities the Brain Gym way:

Tracking[4]

In this Deep Vision[2] variation, the eyes follow a pen, pencil, or finger in the following directions, while the learner presses on both cheekbones at the same time.

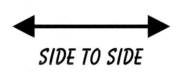

SIDE TO SIDE

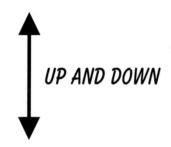

UP AND DOWN

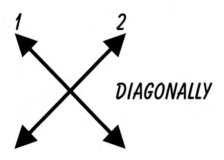

DIAGONALLY

IN A LAZY 8

Using a cup hook, hang a ball from the ceiling on a length of string. Learners then follow the movement of the ball as it swings. Put letters on the ball, and focus on a letter as it is called out.

b k
a j

Visual Convergence

Once again pressing her cheekbones with her fingers, the student lets her eyes follow a pen, finger, or similar object, moving *towards* the nose.

She can do this exercise a few times.

The marvelous Vision Gym^2 exercises described in the chapter on Handwriting make excellent reading tune-ups.

- ✓ **Wake-up Points** - p. 39
- ✓ **Heliotropic Breathing** - p. 39
- ✓ **Butterfly Blinks** - p. 39
- ✓ **Soft Edges** - p. 40
- ✓ **Windows** - p. 41

REMEMBER

Hold cheekbones.

Another playful Vision Gym movement is **The Rainbow**

Stand with arms at sides, shoulder height, palms up.

Breathe in deeply, shoulders back and head to the left, and look past the left hand.

Breathe out, palms facing down, chin dropping to the chest.

Repeat this to the other side.

Whole-Body Midline Integration

The movements we can use for this purpose are:

- ✓ **The Cross Crawl** - p. 6
- ✓ **The Elephant** - p. 26
- ✓ **The Rocker** - p. 22
- ✓ **Cross Crawl Sit-ups** - p. 21

Sight Words

When we are learning to read, we want to memorise some vocabulary as "whole words" or "sight words"

These Brain Gym movements and activities that we use for mastering sight words will also be useful for learning spelling words (see pp. 81-86).

Write the words clearly on flash cards and have fun learning them in the following ways:

Working in pairs, one learner holds the card while the other does the Cross Crawl, looks at the word, and says it aloud.

The Cross Crawl

Use many variations, for example:
marching; the Skip-Across; touching knees, ankles, or toes; to the back; to the side; and while practising saying the word.

Another variation of working in pairs is to look at and say the sight words while doing the Thinking Cap, or doing the Elephant or Lazy 8 movements around the words.

The Thinking Cap

Unroll outer ears from the top down to the earlobes.

The Elephant

"Glue" ear to shoulder. Trace big ∞s around the word as you say it.

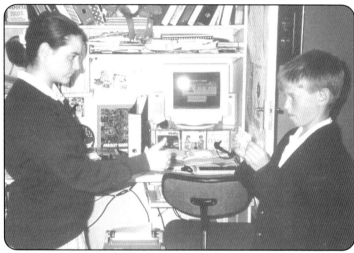

Lazy 8s

Trace ∞s around the word as you say it.

Do **Heliotropic Breathing**[2]

As you inhale, close your eyes. As you exhale, open your eyes and "take a photo" of the word, closing your eyes again as you once again inhale.

In pairs: One partner holds the flash card while the other does any of the **Cross Crawl** variations, then stops to take a Heliotropic Breath and "photo" while at the same time reading the word aloud.

To help some learners, audiotape the words so that they can listen to them while doing the **Cross Crawl/Heliotropic Breathing** routine.

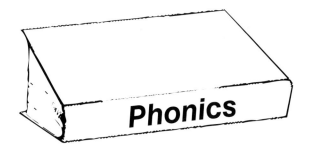

When learning to read with phonics, learners will need to develop the following conceptual skills and abilities:

- Closure (ability to gestalt the whole)
- Visual constancy
- Visual-auditory discrimination
- Figure-ground discrimination
- Auditory and visual memory
- Decoding (word analysis)
- Encoding (blending)
- Recognition of rhythmic clues
- Visual-auditory and motor matching

A Note to Educators

We suggest you use as many senses as possible to aid in the learning of the phonetic sounds involved in reading. Use colours for the phonic "family" groups; **audiotape** the sound blends; **visually** display the phonic word lists; play **games** as further reinforcement, and use **Brain Gym** movements to integrate the visual/auditory/motor correspondences, as on page 77.

We have introduced many of these ideas in other parts of *HANDS ON*.
Choose them and use them!

Brain Gym Movements to Enhance the Senses

AUDITORY

The Thinking Cap - p. 63
The Elephant - p. 26
Neck Rolls - p. 24
The Owl - p. 65
The Footflex - p. 65
The Calf Pump - p. 65
Balance Buttons - p. 68

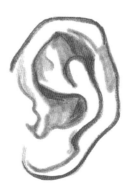

VISUAL

Brain Buttons - p. 6
Balance Buttons - p. 68
Earth Buttons - p. 68
Space Buttons - p. 68
The Energy Yawn - p. 40
Lazy 8s with thumbs - p. 66
Butterfly Blinks - p. 39
Windows - p. 41
Heliotropic Breathing - p. 39
The Wake-up Points - p. 39
The Rainbow - p. 29
Alphabet 8s - p. 45

MEMORY

The Cross Crawl - p. 6
Cross Crawl Sit-ups - p. 21
Think of an X - p. 13
Balance Buttons - p. 68
The Positive Points - p. 62
Neck Rolls - p. 24
The Grounder - p. 78

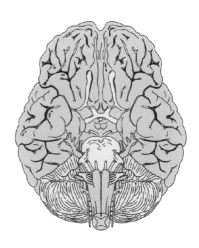

DECODING & ENCODING

⚓ Lazy 8s - p. 25
⚓ The Owl - p. 65
⚓ The Double Doodle - p. 39

+

⚓ The Elephant - p. 26
⚓ The Thinking Cap - p. 63
⚓ Cross Crawl Sit-ups - p. 21

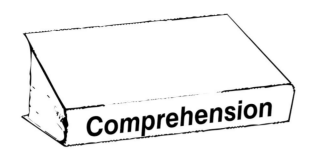

Comprehension

The ability to associate new learning with old, store it, and later retrieve it, is fundamental to reading

It is this ability that makes understanding easier.

Do these Brain Gym movements as part of a reading Tune-up before tests, and before comprehension tasks involving reading, writing, or listening.

✓ **The Footflex** - p. 65

✓ **The Calf Pump** - p. 65

✓ **The Owl** - p. 65

✓ **The Energizer** - p. 79

✓ **The Grounder** - below

✓ **Earth Buttons** - p. 68

✓ **Balance Buttons** - p. 68

✓ **Space Buttons** - p. 68

✓ **The Thinking Cap** - p. 63

✓ **The Positive Points** - p. 62

The Grounder

Legs apart, one foot pointed forward, the other turned out. Bend towards turned-out foot, without extending knee beyond toes. Turn face towards bent knee.

(The boy in the photo is preparing to point his left foot more to the left and turn his face that way too.)

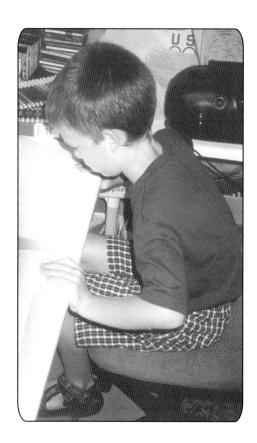

The Energizer

Sit facing a table.
Lower head
towards tabletop,
move forward
and then come
up head first.

Reading Speed

Once we can read, let's bring up our speed to improve fluency, comprehension, and enjoyment!

A quick Brain Gym tune-up includes:

✓ **Lazy 8s** - pp. 37 & 38

✓ **Cross Crawl** - p. 6

✓ **The Owl** - p. 65

✓ **The Calf Pump** - p. 65

✓ **Windows** - p. 41

✓ **Wake-up Points** - p. 39

✓ **Butterfly Blinks** - p. 39

"Reading transports me. I can go anywhere and never leave my chair. It lets me shake hands with new ideas."

—*Rolfe Neill*

Chapter 4

Spelling

Learning how to spell can sometimes be a pain! Here are some ideas for you to make it easier *and* a lot more fun—in class and at home.

Start with PACE . . .
Then do the Brain Gym movements

Rub each ear three times, from the top down to the earlobes.

The Thinking Cap

Some unique ways to learn spelling

The Elephant

Ear "glued" to one shoulder, trace a big Lazy 8 with one arm, then the other arm.

The Owl

Squeeze shoulder muscle. Move head from side to side as far as it can move, while making a sound like the "whoo" of an owl.

Lazy 8s

As you trace the **Lazy 8**, see the word in your mind's eye as you trace around to the left and say the word as you trace around to the right.

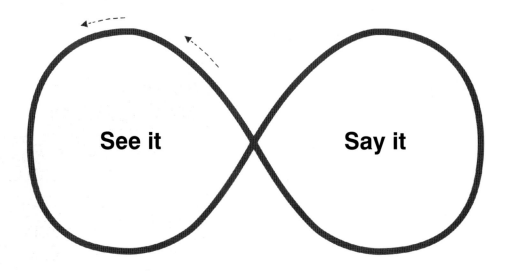

See it   **Say it**

See it . . . say it . . . Now write it

Use **Alphabet 8s** to print the word (example: grasp), as shown on the template on page 58.

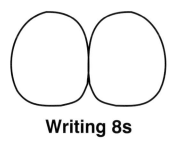

Writing 8s

Do these and notice!

- Do **The Cross Crawl**, looking at the word.

- Do **The Cross Crawl**, looking and spelling the word.

- Do **The Cross Crawl March** (see page 18) and spell the word as you go.

- Do **The Skip-Across** (skipping and at the same time touching opposite knee with opposite hand), as you spell the word.

- Do **The Cross Crawl**, eyes closed, "see" the word, and spell it.

Need a Change of Routine?

Here are some more ideas for you:

- ✍ Write the word using your elbow (**Elbow 8s**^{2}).
- ✍ Write the word using your shoulder.
- ✍ Write the word using your foot.
- ✍ Write the word using **The Elephant**.

TIP:

Place two hoops on floor in the ∞ shape, for child to walk around.

More Ways to Learn Spelling Using Your Whole Brain

The wonderful **Lazy 8s** and **Alphabet 8s** (See Pages 25 and 44 to 49 for an explanation of how to do these movements.)

- ☛ Once the **Alphabet 8s** have been mastered, they can be used to learn spelling. Spell the chosen word by forming the letters of the word in the **Alphabet 8s**.
- ☛ Also while doing the **Lazy 8s** (in the air or on paper), first say the word, then spell it.
- ☛ Hold or massage your **Brain Buttons**; look at a word and spell it.

☞ Write the word on a flash card, then move it in the shape of a **Lazy 8** in front of your face while following it with your eyes. Say the word and spell it.

☞ *Now do this one*
Hold the flash card up to the left of your head. Take a photo of the whole word in your mind (party). Now hold the flash card down to the right side of your body and look at the details of the word (p-ar-ty).

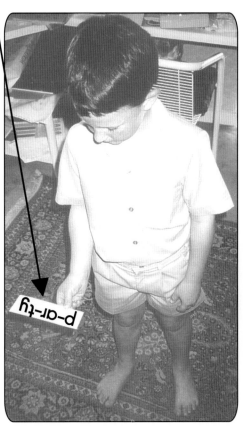

Use Brain Gym movements to help your whole brain learn spelling, and use some of the old favorites as well.

✓ Type out the spelling words on a computer or typewriter (use two hands, please!).
✓ Trace your spelling words in big cursive (connected) letters, using three or four colours and saying the words aloud.
✓ Later, for revision: Put your words on flash cards up on the classroom or bedroom wall and every time you pass a word, spell it!

Chapter 5

Mathematics and Number Concepts

We challenge you!

Once you have familiarised yourselves with the Brain Gym and Vision Gym movements as described in this manual, we challenge *you* to put your mind to devising ways to use the movements in practicing your number concepts.

For example:
A few "teasers" for you.

Counting
(Times tables, counting backwards by 2s, 10s, 100s, etc.)

- Do the **Cross Crawl** while looking at a number line, listening to a tape recording, saying your tables, or counting out loud.
- Walk, skip, or Cross Crawl around the Infinity 8; put on your **Thinking Cap** while listening to a tape recording, or counting and saying your tables out loud.

Numerals
How can you use the **Lazy 8s** to integrate the planning, including direction, of your written numerals? (See page 88 for an example.)

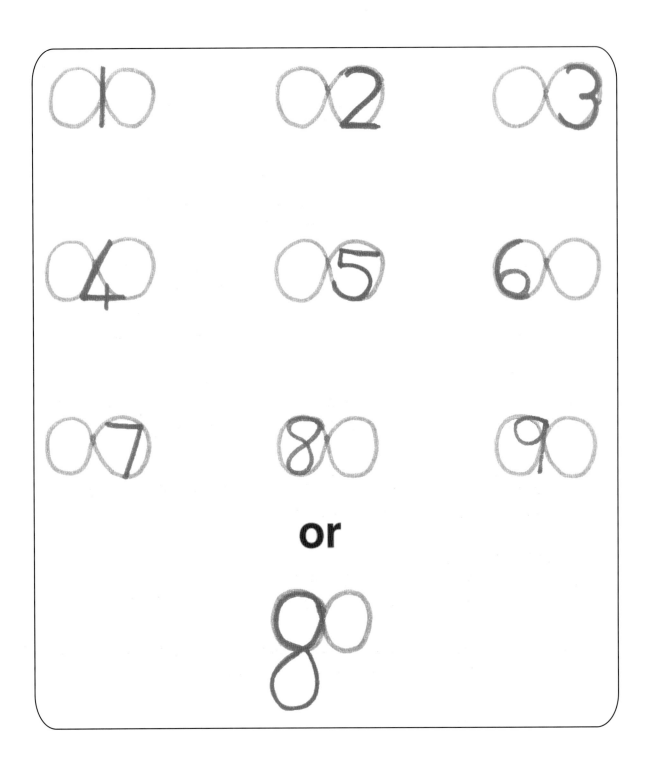

or

Start by doing the ∞ a few times. Then write the numeral in the ∞ as shown in the diagram above.

Chapter 6

The Way Forward

We hope that you enjoy using these ideas in your classroom as much as we have enjoyed putting them together. We know that you are wonderful, innovative, and creative educators!

If you are inspired by the Brain Gym movements as presented in this manual, we invite you to share your ideas with us. We will welcome these as well as your photographs. We are particularly keen to hear your responses to the Mathematics and Number Concept chapter.

Please let us have any feedback you wish to share about your experiences in using this manual, as well as any recommendations and requests you may have. We would so enjoy hearing about your successes!

In your communications with us, please use the email address, fax numbers, and postal addresses listed below.

Email: handson-books@mweb.co.za
Fax: +27-21-797-6204 *or* 083-8-456-0032
Postal Address: P O Box 1019, Sea Point 8060, South Africa

Looking forward to sharing "the way forward" with you, and wishing you a wonderful *HANDS ON* Brain Gym experience!

Marcelle and Isabel

Brain Gym Movements Used in This Manual

Pages

Midline Movements:

The Cross Crawl (and variations)	5, **6**, 8, 10, 13, 16, 17-18, 53, 74, 75, 77, 80, 83, 87
Lazy 8s (and variations)	22, **25**, 26, 27, 28, 32-33, 37-38, 43-51, 54, 55, 56, 57, 66, 69, 70, 74, 75, 77, 80, 82, 83, 84, 85-86, 87, 99, 101
The Double Doodle	**39**, 42, 52, 54, 77
Alphabet 8s	**45-49**, 58, 60, 77, 85
The Elephant	**26**, 37, 50, 55, 64, 73, 74, 75, 77, 82, 84
Neck Rolls	**24**, 55, 64, 77
The Rocker	**22**, 55, 73
Cross Crawl Sit-ups	**21**, 22, 53, 55, 73, 77
The Energizer	78, **79**
Think of an X	**13**, 68, 69, 77

Lengthening Activities:

The Owl	25, 55, **65**, 77, 78, 80, 82
Arm Activation	**31**, 55
The Footflex	**65**, 77, 78
The Calf Pump	30, **65**, 77, 78, 80
The Gravity Glider	**65**
The Grounder	77, **78**

Energy Exercises:

Water	**5**, 8, 9, 10, 12, 14, 16
Brain Buttons	5, **6**, 8, 10, 12, 14, 16, 34, 68, 77, 85
Earth Buttons	35, 55, **68**, 77, 78
Balance Buttons	36, **68**, 77, 78
Space Buttons	35, **68**, 77, 78
The Energy Yawn	**40**, 64, 68, 77
The Thinking Cap	**63**, 74, 77, 78, 81, 87

Deepening Attitudes:

Hook-ups	5, **7**, 8, 13, 15, 16, 19, 62
The Positive Points	**62**, 77, 78

Vision Gym Movements Used in This Manual

APPENDIX 1

APPENDIX 2

APPENDIX 3

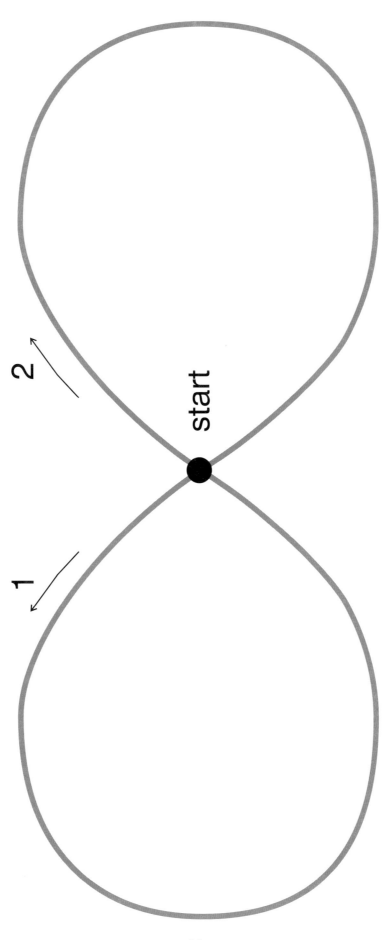

APPENDIX 5

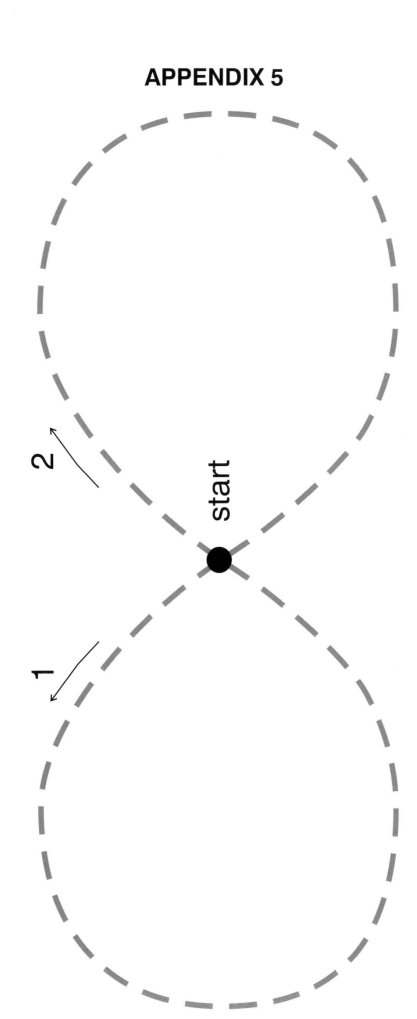

Bibliography

1. Bissinger, Kristen, and Nancy Renfro. *Leap Into Learning! Teaching Curriculum Through Creative Dramatics and Dance.* Austin, Texas: Nancy Renfro Studios, 1990.

2. Dennison, Gail E., and Paul E. Dennison. *Vision Gym: Playful Movements for Natural Seeing.* VAK Verlags GmbH, Kirchzarten bei Freiburg, Germany, 1999.

3. Dennison, Gail E., and Sunny Mello. *Movement Dynamics Teacher's Manual.* Edu-Kinesthetics, Inc., Ventura, California, 1990.*

4. Dennison, Paul E., and Gail E. Dennison. *Brain Gym Handbook.* Edu-Kinesthetics, Inc., Ventura, California, 1989, revised 1997.*

5. Dennison, Paul E., and Gail E. Dennison. *The Dennison Approach to Whole Brain Learning.* Edu-Kinesthetics, Inc., Ventura, California, 1990, revised 2000.*

6. Dennison, Paul E., and Gail E. Dennison. *Brain Gym: Simple Activities for Whole-Brain Learning* and *Brain Gym Teacher's Edition (Revised).* Edu-Kinesthetics, Inc., Ventura, California,1986 and 1994.

7. Edwards, Rita. *Handwriting and Brain Gym Course Manual.* Presented by Rita Edwards at the Post Gathering Course, Colorado Springs, Colorado, 1995.*

8. Edwards, Rita. *Bubble Fun with Brain Gym.* Educational Workshop Mini Publication, Cape Town, South Africa, July 1995.

9. Hannaford, Carla. *Smart Moves: Why Learning Is Not All in Your Head.* Arlington, Virginia: Great Ocean Publishers, 1995.

10. Hawke, Pat. "A Model for Implementing Brain Gym in a School Setting," *Brain Gym Journal*, Vol XII, number 2.

*These course manuals are distributed only to workshop participants.

Publications of Edu-Kinesthetics, Inc.

Brain Gym® by Dennison and Dennison
Brain Gym® *Teacher's Edition* by Dennison and Dennison
Brain Gym® *for Business: Instant Brain Boosters for*
   On-the-Job Success by Teplitz, Dennison and Dennison
Brain Gym® *Surfer* by Sandra Hinsley
Edu-K for Kids by Dennison and Dennison
Hands On: A Practical Photo Manual for Educators, Parents
   and Learners by Isabel Cohen and Marcelle Goldsmith
I am the Child: Using Brain Gym® *with Children Who*
   Have Special Needs by Cecilia Freeman and Gail Dennison
Personalized Whole-Brain Integration by Dennison and Dennison
Switching On: The Whole-Brain Answer to Dyslexia
   by Dr. Paul E. Dennison
Vision Gym®*: Playful Movements for Natural Seeing* (card set
   and booklet) by Dennison and Dennison
A New Paradigm in Reading Instruction (videotape)
   with Dr. Paul E. Dennison
Integrated Movements (audiotape) by Dennison and Dennison

**Visit our www.braingym.com Web site for product descriptions
and pricing.**

Telephone or fax ordering with Visa or MasterCard:
Telephone (805) 650-3303 or toll-free (888) 388-9898
Fax (805) 650-1689
Mail your order to: **Edu-Kinesthetics, Inc.**
Post Office Box 3395, Ventura, California 93006-3395, U.S.A.